GRACE
ON THE
GO

---

101 Quick Ways to Pray

More praise for *Grace on the Go:*

"I recommend Barbara's inspiring reflections to everyone."
—Mary Hynes, Ph.D., Director of Theology, Avila University and author of *Surrender: Pathway to Peace*

"Connecting with God regularly is important to me, but as a busy mom who juggles a demanding career, it's hard to find chunks of time to spend with the Lord. *Grace on the Go* gives me many ideas. I love it! I love it! Barbara is a phenomenal writer." —Halaine Guidry, CSP, MBA, Christian motivational speaker, Baton Rouge, Louisiana

"Barbara offers wisdom, personal experience and warm assurance that God is there to guide us." —Joan Wester Anderson, *New York Times* Best-selling author of *Where Angels Walk* and *Where Miracles Happen*

"Barbara's books soar with hope. Everyone can benefit from her insights." —Antoinette Bosco, columnist and award-winning author of Christian books

Praise for *Nobody's Child Anymore* by Barbara Bartocci:

"A compassionate resource and guide . . . written in a gentle, almost poetic style." —*Today's Librarian*

"Barbara offers practical advice with a lot of heart in it." —*The Washington Post*

GRACE
ON THE
GO

101 Quick Ways to Pray

BARBARA BARTOCCI

MOREHOUSE PUBLISHING

Copyright © 2006 by Barbara Bartocci

All rights reserved. No part of this book may be reproduced, stored in a retrieval system, or transmitted in any form or by any means, electronic, mechanical, including photocopying, recording, or otherwise, without the written permission of the publisher.

Unless otherwise noted, the Scripture quotations contained herein are from the New Revised Standard Version Bible, copyright © 1989 by the Division of Christian Education of the National Council of Churches of Christ in the U.S.A. Used by permission. All rights reserved.

Morehouse Publishing, P.O. Box 1321, Harrisburg, PA 17105

Morehouse Publishing, 445 Fifth Avenue, New York, NY 10016

Morehouse Publishing is an imprint of Church Publishing Incorporated.

Cover design by Brenda Klinger
Interior design by Irene Zevgolis

Library of Congress Cataloging-in-Publication Data

Bartocci, Barbara.
 Grace on the go : 101 quick ways to pray / Barbara Bartocci.
  p. cm.
 ISBN-13: 978-0-8192-2230-5 (pbk.)
 1. Prayer—Christianity. I. Title.
 BV215.B378 2006
 248.3'2—dc22
          2006004860

Printed in the United States of America

06 07 08 09 10 9 8 7 6 5 4 3 2

To my beloved granddaughter Isabella.
May your life be filled with grace.

Contents

Acknowledgments ix
Hurried Beginnings 1
Part I: Living Each Day with God 5
Waking Up 7
At Work 17
Meals on the Run 33
At Home with Family 37
Personal Behavior 43
Building Relationships 61
When Times Are Stressful 71
In the Evening 85
Part II: If You Have a Couple More Minutes 91
Time Out: A Couple of Extra Minutes with God 93
Notes 97

Acknowledgments

Many thanks to Andrea Warren, Deborah Shouse, and Sony Hocklander for their watchful eyes as I wrote this book. Special appreciation also goes to Jennifer, my spiritual director at Shantivanam House of Prayer, and to Fr. Rob Lord, rector at St. Michael and All Angels Episcopal Church, whose teachings on prayer have meant so much.

Hurried Beginnings

My daughter, Sony Hocklander, grabbed a sneaker, told one son to put on his jacket, shuttled the dog out the kitchen door, and reminded her youngest, "Get your lunch money." She called up the stairs to her husband, Kevin, "Don't forget to pick up the groceries!" and after simultaneously stacking dishes in the dishwasher while answering her cordless phone, she began pawing through her purse, muttering, "Where are my keys? Has anyone seen my car keys?"

Does this sound like a morning at your house?

Meanwhile, at my own home, I rushed around, too. I finished packing for a business trip and gathered my notes for a seminar I was scheduled to give the next day. Hurriedly, I watered the plants, grabbed my exercise clothes (just enough time for aerobics class before I left for the airport), checked e-mail, made two phone calls, then headed for the gym, remembering to drop off dry cleaning and stop for gas en route. In a different way, I was as busy as my daughter. Still, as busy as I was, and as jam-packed as my life had become, something seemed to be missing.

Is life too hectic for prayer?

I wanted to deepen my spiritual life, to do more than attend church on Sunday or dash off the evening prayers I'd learned in childhood. I wanted to bring into my life—24/7—a more profound sense of God's presence. But for a long time, finding more time for God in my hectic life seemed overwhelming. It was like losing those last five pounds. I had great plans to do it, but never seemed to get it done.

Then it occurred to me that living more spiritually is like any other seemingly daunting task. The way to do it is to break it into bite-size pieces. And I realized that "living spiritually" is not something that exists *out there*. It's a commitment to make our lives—*as they unfold*—a gift to God.

This is hardly a new idea. It exists in every religion, eastern and western. But it's an idea with special meaning for Christians. Because Jesus Christ taught that the kingdom of heaven is within, every act—every task in our ordinary day—is potentially holy if we do it with right intent. Our days are filled with moments of grace—encounters with God's infinite love and mercy—if only we learn to look for them.

Finding grace right where you are

I'm writing this book for anyone who feels as busy as my daughter and me. Whether you're thirty or fifty, if you're

Hurried Beginnings

continually on the go, juggling a dozen different demands, yet yearning to deepen your spiritual life, you'll find in this book some *practical* and *imaginative* ways to put a spiritual spin on your ordinary day.

Sometimes it only takes a minute. I call these sixty-second encounters with grace "one-minute prayers." And since a relationship with God is always like a two-step dance—one step going *inward* in prayer and another step going *outward* in loving action—I've also included some short reflections to ponder that each contain an action step. You might call them mini-retreats.

I hope you won't try to read *Grace on the Go* from front to back, and then set it aside on your bookshelf. It's meant to be something you keep handy, to refer to over and over again. Open it at any page and see what "speaks" to you. Or, since I've divided the book into sections the way we usually divide our days, open it to the time of day you're in at that moment. See what awaits you.

And notice the blank pages at the end of the book. These are for you. Use your imagination to jot down your own unique "one-minute prayers." Or, as you become more aware of God's grace occurring daily in your life, journal a few reflections of your own.

I'd love to have you share with me some of your grace-on-the-go experiences. So if you like, e-mail me at BBartocci@sbcglobal.net.

And now let's begin the way we begin each day. With a wake-up call.

Part I:
Living Each Day with God

Waking Up

⏰ 1. Give an alarm-clock alleluia

When your alarm goes off in the morning, open your eyes and repeat this line from the Psalms: "This is the day the Lord has made. Let us rejoice and be glad." Commit to living in gratitude for the day, and you'll soon notice how much happier your day is.

⏰ 2. Pray with your snooze button

My friend Annie has an alarm clock with a snooze-reminder that goes off ten minutes after the initial *rrrring*. When her alarm goes off, she sits up in bed without turning on the light and breathes slowly and deeply. "I pay attention to each breath, to my heartbeat, to the feel of my skin against the sheets. I don't plan my day. I merely sit prayerfully in the early morning quiet. It centers me." When her snooze-reminder gives its ten-minute buzz, she turns on the light and goes about her usual morning business.

⏰ 3. Accept today's reality

Ken, a sixty-five-year-old acquaintance, said to me, with a touch of melancholy, "I'm just now realizing I never appreciated how happy I was when I was happy." Oh, what a sad realization! And yet it happens. We get so caught up in the "If only's," so focused on the past or the future, that we forget to look for the gift in the life we're living now.

Here's a wonderful affirmation that helps me come back to the day at hand. Say it out loud as you're climbing out of bed: "I is where I is." Yes! Wishing I were someplace else won't change a darn thing. So sing it! Shout it! "I IS WHERE I IS." Don't waste precious life energy wishing you could be someplace else. Ask God to help you appreciate right where you are today. For the next twenty-four hours, vow to live in the reality of what *is*, accepting everything in your life as a gift—both the good and the seemingly bad—because even apparent problems offer opportunities to grow.

⏰ 4. Floss and pray

Are you like me, eager to grab a toothbrush and tackle "morning mouth"? A local dentist once spoke at our church about the way God had moved in his life. As he concluded, he said, with a smile, "Every day do two important things: floss—and pray." His audience laughed but I never forgot his words. As you floss and brush your teeth, prayerfully ask for the grace to use your mouth in ways that reflect God, by speaking only words of love in the coming day.

Waking Up

⏰ 5. Practice shower-power

Water is a powerful spiritual symbol. As you soap and rinse in the shower this morning, pray to be cleansed from any feelings of anger, bitterness, resentment, or regret. Recall the words of Isaiah (58:11): "The Lord will guide you continually. . . . You shall be like a watered garden, like a spring of water, whose waters never fail."

⏰ 6. Walk the dog

There's no better excuse for some reflective time than strolling around the block waiting for your pet to do its duty. I have a little "rescue dog" that I got at the animal shelter, and if I'm in bed and Sandie licks my hand, I know I'd better get up or she'll make an accident on the rug. So I pull on a jacket, grab her leash, and we head outdoors. While Sandie stops and sniffs the world around her, I, too, stop and pay attention to God's glorious world around me. (If you don't have a dog, you could always offer to walk your neighbor's.)

⏰ 7. Exult in tulips

Where I live, a springtime walk shows a riot of tulips and jonquils and daffodils, red and yellow and purple—giddy, joyful flags that proclaim, "New life is here!" To get tulips in the spring, you plant bulbs in the fall. Though my friend Mary wasn't an experienced gardener, she bought three dozen bulbs, dug down eight to ten inches, added potting soil, and then, to make sure she'd done everything right, double-checked with a gardener friend. Immediately the gardener asked, "Did you plant the bulbs *face up*?"

"Bulbs have faces?" blurted Mary.

Like Mary, *I* never knew bulbs have faces. What if Mary hadn't talked to her gardener friend? She could have planted all her bulbs face down, and in the spring not a single tulip would have bloomed. Then Mary might have said, disappointment edging her voice, "Well, God didn't intend me to

God's plan	My blunder	God's reweave
I am a loving Parent.	*Inconsistent discipline. Scoldings that hurt my child's self image.*	*A combination of prayer, sincere desire, and counseling help me learn more effective parenting techniques.*
I am a compassionate disciple of Christ.	*I get so self-engrossed and in such a hurry, I forget to pay attention to others, and sometimes walk right over their needs.*	*I slow down enough to truly listen and observe the needs of others.*

have tulips." But God had nothing to do with it.

Mary's experience made me wonder: How many times have I incompletely managed one of life's projects and then blamed the disappointing results on God, as in "I guess it wasn't God's will"? Can you think of a consequence in your life that you referred to as God's will? Can you look back now with wiser eyes and see your own contribution to the choice you made or the action you took? "As you sow, so shall you reap," says Scripture. Part of grace-in-action means using our God-given powers to reason and think, and, if disappointing consequences occur, to learn and grow.

8. Watch for spider webs

Sometimes my friend Terri and I exercise-walk in a nearby park, and often we use the time to talk about our spiritual journeys. One Friday, we were so busy talking that we walked—*splat!*—into a large spider web. As Terri brushed away the strands of web that clung to her hair and eyelashes, she mused aloud, "God's plans for us are a lot like spider webs, aren't they? Beautifully fashioned until we blunder into them, ripping and tearing them because we failed to look. But God, just like his creature the spider, is able to reweave every web that we destroy." Only Terri could find a spiritual metaphor in the yucky feeling of a spider web splattered across her face!

Still, her spider-web image stayed with me. A few days later, I even made a little table:

What I noticed is that God's reweaving seems to involve my active involvement. Think about recent events in your life. Can you see how you might have torn apart a beautiful plan that God had in mind for you? How can you assist God in the reweaving?

9. Reflect kindness

My friend Bev doesn't walk. She jogs, even in the winter when it's dark and cold at six in the morning. She used to jog past a large construction site where workers were usually milling about. One morning, a big, burly worker accosted her. "Uh-oh," thought Bev. But with a grin, the man held out an orange reflector vest. "Lady, you're not safe, running in the dark the way you do. The guys and me, we got a little worried, so we bought you this."

Talk about love in action! Do you know someone who seems to be stumbling in the dark? Pray for grace to show as much kindness as those construction workers showed Bev. You might even resolve to do something kind for someone who brings out the darkness in you by rubbing you the wrong way. Then notice how difficult it is to make yourself do it.

10. Prepare to wait

"Hurry up and wait" is an old Army saying, but we all know how irritating it is to be stuck in a long line at the supermarket or be forced to sit in one of those little exam rooms at a doctor's office. Instead of tapping your toe in frustration, try this:

Waking Up

keep tucked in your purse or briefcase a book of spiritual wisdom, one you can pull out and read in small bites. A pocket edition of the New Testament, a book of Psalms and Proverbs, William Barclay's *Growing in Christian Faith* or *The Imitation of Christ* (Or even *Grace on the Go*!) Instead of fuming because the person ahead of you is taking forever, use the moment to place yourself in the presence of God.

Once, while impatiently waiting for a coworker who was late, I pulled out the travel Bible I keep in my purse. It fell open to a page in Proverbs and this is what I read: "A gentle answer turns away wrath, but a harsh word stirs up anger." I'd been ready to chew out my colleague because he'd kept me waiting, but the wise words in Proverbs 15 prompted me to take a deep breath and calm down. (Simultaneously I also remembered that the first descriptive word in 1 Corinthians 13 says "Love is *patient*.") When my colleague arrived, full of apologies because he'd been delayed by his boss, he found me relaxed and smiling, and we accomplished a lot in a very short time.

11. Practice driveway meditation

> "Is prayer your steering wheel or your spare tire?" Corrie Ten Boom

Do you commute to work? Turn it into a time for prayer. Before starting the car engine, place your hands lightly on the steering wheel and breathe deeply several times. Ask the Holy

Spirit to steer you through your day. Back out of your driveway slowly, aware of the slowness, and then drive in a conscious, quiet fashion to your workplace. Instead of mentally making your to-do list as you drive, think about your *to-be* list. Let words like *compassionate*, *kind*, *serene*, and *diligent* percolate through your mind, giving you grace-filled thoughts to carry you in a loving manner through the day.

⏰ 12. Turn off your radio and cell phone

So often we drive on automatic pilot while we talk on our portable phones or listen to jingly radio commercials. How long has it been since you paid attention to the actual act of driving, to the feel of the road, the weather outside, the sights and sounds around you? If possible, avoid the whizzing freeway for a change and take back roads, even if it adds a few minutes to the commute. (But stay away from streets crowded with the frustration of traffic lights and stop-and-go traffic.) In the quiet of your car, be mindful of the moment. Feel thankful.

I have a few short prayers I like to repeat as I drive. One is the line from the Psalms: "Praise the Lord, o my soul." Or simply, "Lord have mercy, Christ have mercy, Lord have mercy, Christ have mercy." I find that my mentally murmured prayers make a peaceful "hum" that fits in nicely with the hum of my tires on the road. It's so much better than listening to news of the latest murders, traffic deaths, or terrorist threats.

⏰ 13. Pump in the spirit

Need gas on your way to work? As you pump, visualize God's spirit flowing into you, filling you with enough holy energy to do God's will for the rest of the day. What is God's will? Jesus tells us we're called to love one another. Yes, that even includes the driver who almost cuts you off as you're making a turn out of the gas station.

At Work

⏰ 14. Re-define Success

Penny is vice president of a large bank and is always on local lists of "successful women." But one day we met for coffee, and over latte she mused, "What if life isn't about my business success but only about how kind I am when no one else is watching?" I was particularly stopped by her phrase, "when no one else is watching." Our society is always after us to go for the prize. Succeed! Be noticed! I've done it myself: I once titled a business article, "Color Yourself Visible."

It's important to remind ourselves, as Penny did, that God's definition of success is quite different from ours. While we busily collect our kudos, God observes our acts of personal kindness, especially when no one "important" is around. Jesus put it quite succinctly: "Beware of practicing your piety before others in order to be seen by them. . . . So whenever you give alms, do not sound a trumpet before you. . . . But when you give alms, do not let your left hand know what your right hand is doing, so that your alms may be done in secret" (Matt 6:1–4). Today, perform some small act of random kindness—and make sure you do it when no one else is looking.

⏰ 15. CLIMB STAIRS

A lot of us work in multi-story buildings. If you work on an upper floor, skip the elevator and climb the stairs. It's good for your body *and* for your soul. Climb thoughtfully, breathing slowly and using the time alone to experience your connection with God. Pause at each landing, not only to catch your breath, but also to focus for a moment on one of the blessings in your life. Say "thanks" before continuing your climb.

⏰ 16. OFFER AN ELEVATOR BLESSING

No stairs? Next time you share an elevator with someone, silently ask God to meet that person's unique needs. Add a smile of your own.

⏰ 17. LET GO OF BEING *RIGHT*

Joe is a human resources manager who told me there are four magic words that can lower the decibel-level in any heated discussion: *You may be right*. It's a great phrase because you're not saying, "You *are* right," only acknowledging that possibility. Why is it so hard to release our need to be right? I'm reminded of a cartoon caption: "Don't confuse me with facts; my mind is made up." Yet isn't the essence of empathy a willingness to acknowledge, now and then, "*You* may be right"? A prayer I learned in childhood says, "Jesus meek and humble of heart, make my heart like unto thine."

Surely a humble heart can say, "You may be right." Look for a valid occasion to use this expression at work or at home. Observe the response you get.

⏰ 18. Say the count-to-sixty-avoid-a-fight prayer

Is it too late to say, "You may be right"?

Have your emotions taken over so you're ready to burst out in anger? Angry words are often regretted later. Next time someone pushes your hot button, count to sixty before you respond, using these words, "one-for-God, two-for-God, three-for-God," and so on.

⏰ 19. Try prayerful single-tasking

It's become a workplace axiom that multi-tasking is a good thing. We try to cram at least two things into every minute. (Sometimes three: I saw a woman putting on lipstick as she talked on her cell phone and drove past me on the freeway.) But a growing body of research shows that multi-tasking actually erodes productivity. Even dividing your time between two simple tasks, such as reading e-mail while talking on the phone, has been shown to lower comprehension and concentration. And switching from one job to another before you complete the first is never as productive as completing one task and then moving on.

One reason for chronic multi-tasking is that we all feel too busy. Working moms juggle the "second shift" at home. In companies experiencing layoffs or hiring freezes or both, the remaining workers are handed additional tasks and are afraid to say, "No."

Let me suggest the one form of multi-tasking that is really effective. Do one thing at a time—but do it prayerfully. As you begin, offer your work as a prayerful gift to God. Ask for the grace to do it meaningfully and *without anxiety*.

I like the phrase coined by Jean-Pierre de Caussade, an eighteenth-century French priest who spoke of "the sacrament of the present moment." He said, "Grace is the will of God . . . acting in the center of our hearts when we . . . are occupied in other ways."[1] He urged his adherents not to worry about outcomes but simply to follow the example of St. Paul and say, in every moment, "Lord, what should I do?"

Then—and this is the key—have faith that what you are doing at this moment *is* the will of God. Give it your devoted attention. Don't try to mix-and-match tasks. You can start small. For *one hour*, prayerfully perform one task at a time. Try to complete it before you move on. Too hard? Your attention is wandering? You're being interrupted? Then start even smaller. Can you single-task prayerfully for at least five minutes? Try it.

⏰ 20. Offer telephone thanksgivings

Instead of looking at phone calls as interruptions, let your telephone remind you of the blessings God so richly bestows. Every time your phone rings, recall something good in your life and say a brief prayer of thanks before you answer. If it's

At Work

been "one of those days," say thanks anyway because sometimes we learn the most from life's challenges.

21. Computerize your devotions

Like many who work in customer service, Marie occasionally has to cope with agitated, angry customers. She told me she programmed her computer screensaver to read "Everyone is a God-holder" because "It reminds me that everyone holds within themselves the spirit of God. So even when someone is giving me a hard time, I try to listen and respond to the divine spark within that person." Mother Teresa said it in a slightly different way: "Seek the face of God in everything, everyone, everywhere all the time—[by] seeing and adoring the presence of Jesus."[2]

To keep her message from becoming stale, now and then Marie changes it. "Thank you, God, for everything" and, "This is the day the Lord has made" are two other favorites.

Before opening her e-mail, Hillary goes to www.sacredspace.ie/ for the morning prayers posted by an Irish community. Jamie likes the Christian prayer links at www.beliefnet.com and www.ChristianityToday.com. Another friend of mine gets her daily inspiration on www.DailyGuideposts.com. Praying with some help from a website is a great way to start your work day. If you Google the phrase "Christian prayer sites," you'll have 7 million to choose from!

⏰ 22. Make God your boss

Betty was in her early fifties when her department acquired a new supervisor. He nitpicked and complained no matter how carefully she did her work. Betty didn't want to quit—she'd already put in too many years with her company—but she was reaching a boiling point. Then she figured out a unique way to handle her situation.

"I fired my boss," she said, "and went to work directly for God."

"Really?" I couldn't help but smile. "What kind of boss is God?"

"Very reasonable," said Betty. "God requires just two things: One, I have to do my best—despite my frustrations—because God will know if I don't. And two, that's *all* I have to do. No matter what anyone else says. God requires no more."

Are you in a similar situation? Would it help to mentally "fire" your boss and go to work directly for God? Try it for a day.

⏰ 23. Dare to soar

At a creative conference I attended, participants were asked to write a poem, attach it to a helium balloon, and send it aloft into the sky, to land who knew where. We could have taken home our balloons (and our poems) and tied them to the bedpost, but in the end, the balloons would have shriveled and we'd have lost them anyway. As the workshop leader pointed

AT WORK

out, "Isn't that our choice in life? To tie ourselves to bedposts or to soar into Mystery?"

Another name for God is "Mystery." Today, do something out of the ordinary. Drive to work a different way. Invite someone to lunch that you'd like to know better. Read a magazine that holds a political view different from yours. Offer the experience to God as a way of soaring, if just a little, into Mystery.

24. BE KIND TO COWORKERS

Get in the habit of performing small kindnesses for coworkers. Do little extras that don't take a lot of time, but will be appreciated. Drop off a colleague's copies from the copy machine, saving him a walk. Get a cup of coffee for someone else when you're going for a cup of your own. Let a coworker know about a helpful website you've found. When you hear a compliment about a colleague or notice a job well done, pass on the compliment. Better yet, write a note.

Albert Schweitzer said, "Constant kindness can accomplish much. As the sun makes ice melt, kindness causes misunderstanding, mistrust and hostility to evaporate."[3]

I observed that in my own workplace some years ago. Our department had become very acrimonious. Then we acquired a new supervisor who, among other kindly habits, kept coupons for ice cream cones in her desk drawer. Whenever someone finished a tough project or was celebrating a special occasion, she'd drop off an ice cream coupon. Her kindness was so contagious, the whole department caught it, and just as Dr. Schweitzer said, hostility evaporated.

Start your kindness habit today. You can start small.

25. CHANGE YOUR PERSPECTIVE

I live in a city that spans two states—Kansas and Missouri—and the road between the two is called, naturally enough, State Line Road. In a workshop I attended, the audience was asked, "What is the function of State Line Road?" Hands went up, and the replies were all the same: "State Line Road divides the two states." Tom Jacobs, our workshop leader, smiled. "Isn't it also the point at which the two states *connect*?"

The day after Tom's workshop, I showed my creative portfolio to an advertising executive I was hoping would hire me for a project. I was proud of my eclectic sampler, but he shook his head disdainfully. "Your work seems scattered to me. There's too much variety. As if you're not quite sure what you want to be when you grow up." His patronizing tone felt like a total put-down. I was devastated when I left his office.

Driving home, I crossed State Line Road. Suddenly I smiled, remembering how I'd learned there were two different ways to view the road. The next day, I wrote a letter to the executive in which I said, "You called the variety of my work scattered. I believe it shows an unusually wide range and depth of experience." He never responded, but I didn't care. What mattered was the inner power I'd found to reverse a demoralizing comment. For that, I thanked God (and Tom).

At Work

Has something occurred in your life that could be seen from more than one perspective? Ask God to help you choose the most life-affirming view.

⏰ 26. Try to be like . . .

When I ran my ad agency, one of my favorite clients was a suburban bank president. Earl was an astute businessman, but he also treated customers and employees in a very personal, caring way. He wore an unusual ring on his right hand, gold with a small diamond, and one day I asked him about it.

"The diamond is from my mother's engagement ring," he explained. "My dad died young and we were stone cold poor in Wichita, Kansas, so periodically, Mom would take her diamond ring to Mr. Frisbein's pawn shop and pawn it for what she needed: $50 or $100. What she really got was a secured loan, because Mr. Frisbein never sold the family heirlooms people brought to him. It became the kids' responsibility—all four of us—to help earn enough to retrieve Mom's ring. The next time we needed help, though, back it went to Mr. Frisbein." Earl paused. "I try to run my bank the way Mr. Frisbein ran his pawn shop."

Earl followed the values of someone he admired. In your workplace, whose values are grounded in the Gospel? Think of one thing you might do today to emulate the values of that person.

Grace on the Go

⏰ 27. Refresh yourself

If you're feeling tired today, it's probably because you are. Our 24/7 lives mean many people are chronically sleep-deprived. In fact, a poll of adult Americans found that 63 percent sleep fewer than eight hours a night, and Europeans don't fare much better.

In Matthew's gospel, Jesus stopped at a well where a Samaritan woman was drawing water. When you first read it, the focus appears to be on his interchange with the woman, but I also noticed this line: "Jesus was tired from the journey." I thought, "Hmmm. Even Jesus grew tired now and then." If he took time to rest at the well, why can't I? Or you? It's so common to "burn the midnight oil" in our fast-paced society that we feel guilty if we admit we're tired or would like a little time to simply "veg."

But sometimes the best way to pray is to find time for "being" instead of "doing." What represents a well where you can refresh yourself? Picture it now in your mind. Give yourself permission to go there, whether it's a physical place (a lakeside park near home or a soothing soak in the bathtub) or a place of mental refreshment (a few minutes on your own to read). Then spend a little time there with God, in quiet prayer and reflection.

⏰ 28. Practice holy curiosity

A September 2005 issue of *Harvard Business Review* said, "As a society we are biased toward answers. Answers settle matters and tell us it's safe to move forward. Questions are troublemakers, poking holes in ideas and plans."⁴ But Albert Einstein said: "The important thing is not to stop questioning. Curiosity has its own reason for existence. Never lose your *holy* curiosity."

What a wonderful combination of words! *Holy curiosity*. Our ability to wonder, to inquire, to welcome what is new, and to keep our minds open to truth when and where we find it—surely this is one of the most miraculous qualities that human beings possess. Maintain an open mind today. Ask questions. Acknowledge truth when you find it. Pray to be led by holy curiosity.

⏰ 29. LIVE YOUR DREAMS *NOW*

Dave was an attorney who often worked seventy or eighty hours a week. When I interviewed him for a magazine article, I was struck by something he said: "I'm pretty burned out by my work," he confided, "but in ten years I'll have enough set aside so I can retire. Then I'll look for what I *really* like to do." I found myself thinking about the gospel story in Luke 12:20. Jesus described a rich man who planned to build bigger barns to store all his riches so that *someday* he could relax and take life easy. God responded, "You fool! This very night your life will be demanded of you."

How peculiarly human for us to see our lives extending into some limitless horizon, and to imagine that we can set aside our riches (and our dreams) with a guarantee that we'll have a chance to pursue them "later." *What if later never comes?* Are you doing what you really want to do, using the talents God has blessed you with so richly? If you can't pursue your dream on a grand scale, then dream locally. Paint watercolors on the weekend. Use your singing talent in a local civic chorus. Enroll in one college class at night. But don't *wait* to pursue what you like to do. Glorify God with your talents *now*. None of us knows when life will make its final demand.

30. GO THE EXTRA MILE

Lauraine, my insurance broker, is so tenacious she won't take no for an answer. When Ted came to her for help, he'd been turned down by three other health insurance companies because of a pre-existing heart condition. Lauraine refused to give up. She kept making phone calls until she found him coverage. "I put so much time into it, I only netted $34," she told me. But her smile made it clear that earning money wasn't her primary motive. "Go not one mile but two," said Jesus. I wondered how willing I am to go the extra mile for someone, especially if it nets me just $34? Think about someone who went the extra mile for you. What was the cost in time, money, or effort? When did you last extend yourself for someone? Stay alert to opportunities to go the extra mile. Notice if you choose to do it. Don't judge yourself. Just notice.

At Work

⏰ 31. Touch the earth

Native Americans have this saying: "Never let a day go by without touching the earth with your foot." Notice the word is *earth*—not cement or indoor-outdoor carpeting.

Even if it's only a couple of times a week, take a five- or ten-minute break and walk outside the building where you work. Walk in a meditative way—give up your usual energized stride to pay attention to the movement of lifting your leg, bending your knee, and placing your foot. Walking meditatively means walking slowly at a pace that allows you to observe your breathing and your body. Look around. Notice the squirrels, the bark on trees, the variety of leaves. Listen to the sounds you're usually too busy to hear. Nature tunes us into God's presence, even in the city. All we have to do is step outside. And touch the earth.

⏰ 32. Climb off your camel

The Southwest desert has always appealed to me: the beauty of the distant mountains, the wide expanse of sky, the rugged desolation of the land. On a recent trip, I was enjoying the solitude until I drove into a desert town. A festival was underway and the streets were crowded with RVs, campers, and carnival rides. But what really hooked me was the live camel race. Two camels were lurching awkwardly down a makeshift racetrack, kicking up dust and spitting green bile. Maybe it was their almost comical clumsiness, but it made me think about my own daily camel race. "Too much to do! Can't pray today!" I cry, and off I run. Or lurch. Yet Jesus—and Old Testament prophets—felt a recurring need to retreat to the desert to pray. Why should I be any different?

What is your camel race? See if you can climb off your beast, even if it's only for five minutes. Leave your desk and go into an unused conference room. Walk outdoors. Or even—as one woman did—retreat to a stall in the restroom. Once you're alone, breathe deeply several times. Mentally say, "Be still, and know I am God" (Psalm 46:10, NIV). Say it again, shortening it each time. "Be still and know I am." "Be still and know." "Be still." And finally, "Be." If you must climb back on your camel, don't forget the power to *be*.

33. SKIP THE E-MAIL

It's a good thing St. Paul liked to write letters. Where would the Christian church be without them? If Paul were living today, I'm sure he would appreciate e-mail. It's great for quickly spreading the word and connecting us instantly with friends and colleagues around the globe.

But St. Paul reminded his readers, "You yourselves are our letter, written on our hearts, to be known and read by all; and you show that you are a letter of Christ, prepared by us, written not with ink but with the Spirit of the living God, not on tablets of stone but on tablets of human hearts" (2 Corinthians 3:2–3). In the same spirit, some occasions call for more than e-mail. They call for a face-to-face meeting where we can dialogue and add body language to our message.

At Work

Or they call for the old-fashioned written word. Love letters written on note paper can be reread years later. Condolence letters remind the bereaved, "You are not alone in missing your beloved." A written thank-you conveys a depth of appreciation that telephoned words lack. Letters of apology are perhaps hardest to write, but sometimes we can put on paper words that stick in our throat when we try to say them.

Next time you sit down to write an e-mail, ask yourself, "Is this an e-mail occasion?" Or should you leave your computer and become a personal "letter from Christ"? Or it is more appropriate to send a note by postal mail? If you do choose the latter, always add a silent blessing as you stamp your letter.

Meals on the Run

⏰ **34. Say grace**

"Cleaning up *my* dining room means picking up the fast food wrappers off the floor of my car," said a friend. I laughed, but it's true. A lot of families eat on the run these days, especially when kids are involved in sports or other activities. Eating on different schedules or out in public makes it easy to lose the habit of saying grace before meals. But in Cincinnati, my stepson Marc, his wife Carol, and their teenage son Joel say grace even if they're in a restaurant. "Giving thanks three times a day is our way of putting God first," says Carol.

How about your next meal? While you're unwrapping your hamburger, take a moment to consciously say thanks.

⏰ **35. Try lunchbox communion**

Maybe you're so busy at work, you eat at your desk while you're doing something else. Today, for at least one minute, *stop!* Set aside whatever else you're working on and focus on your eating. Chew each bite slowly and deliberately. Notice the taste and texture of what you eat—the crunch of celery, the nutty chewiness of whole-wheat bread, the smooth sweetness of yogurt—and as you eat, give thanks for the incredible abundance of food in this country. Be in communion with all those who provide food and ask God to bless them. And ask a special blessing for those who are hungry.

36. Fast for one-minute

I could live the rest of my life without eating french fries or potato chips. But I'm a sucker for chocolate and sugar. What's your particular food weakness? When you're stressed, are you tempted to eat something you know isn't good for you? Try this. Wait *one minute*. Offer the minute to God and ask for the grace you need to control your appetite. Chances are you'll no longer be tempted when the minute is up. And if you do give in—well, God forgives you, so forgive yourself.

37. Start a brown bag hour of power

At the insurance company where Lauraine worked, a chance discussion led several colleagues to form a once-a-month brown bag hour of spiritual sharing. "We come from different denominations, but what we have in common is a desire to practice in the workplace the teachings of Christ," says Lauraine. She and her coworkers take turns as group leaders, assign reading in various books, and discuss their own personal challenges as they try to live Christian principles on the job.

Meals on the Run

At the end of each meeting, the group spends a few minutes in silent prayer.

⏰ 38. Cook up a memory

I seldom need recipes for everyday cooking, but one day I went searching for a curry recipe because I hadn't made it in a long time. My cookbook was a hodgepodge. Stuffed inside were 3 x 5 note cards, many splashed with grease, including one titled, "Mrs. McBride's shrimp casserole." Why, she was the mother of my best friend in high school! Another, "Nancy Smith's cheesecake," referred to a neighbor I knew as a young Navy wife. I found a note in my deceased mother's handwriting, and traced my fingers gently across her words. As I thumbed through more recipes, I was flooded with delicious memories. Next time you cook, pay attention to the memories that are sparked by the dishes you make. Bless all those who sweeten your recollections, thanking God for the spiritual nourishment these people have brought to your life.

⏰ 39. Sprinkle salt

In our neighborhood, if you pay an extra dollar, the trash company gives you a green box to put your recyclables in. Jesus told his disciples, "You are the salt of the earth" (Matthew 5:13). He used this metaphor because salt is so necessary to human life. And if we're the earth's salt, surely this means our attentive caretaking is essential to maintaining this wonderful blue and green planet on which we live. Do you recycle? Do you support "green" legislation? As you sprinkle salt on your food, ask yourself, "Am I doing enough as a caretaker of our blessed, God-given environment?"

⏰ 40. Eat an artichoke

While living in northern California near Salinas, known as the Artichoke Capital of the World, I became a fan of this odd-looking vegetable. To eat an artichoke, you pull off each leaf, dip it in melted butter, savor its taste, and then toss the leaf. If you don't discard the leaves, you'll never reach the succulent, delicious heart of the artichoke.

Writer Thomas Merton defined sanctity as a movement from the false self to the true self. I think eating artichokes is nature's metaphor for doing just that. We pull off the outer leaves (our false selves) in order to reach the heart (our true self).

Take a minute to ponder what you might discard from your life. Are you letting superficial status symbols define your self worth? Do negative childhood messages rule your adult life? Do fears hold you back from taking a risk that will help you grow? "Sanctity is nothing more than becoming ourselves," said Merton. Pray for the grace to be committed to the vocation God has given you to be yourself.

At Home with Family

⏰ 41. Pray a peanut butter minute

This is a good one for moms of school kids, and it's very simple. When you make sandwiches for your child's lunch, whisper a prayer into the lunch pail. You might even tuck in a blessing on a post-it note.

⏰ 42. Pray with your children

After dinner, Mike and Lois gather in a circle with their three kids for family prayer. "First, we say the Lord's Prayer very slowly together," said Lois. "Then each of the kids takes turns saying 'Thank you, God, for . . .' followed by 'I ask God, for . . .' At the end, all together, we say, 'We love you, Jesus.'" Sure, admits Lois, there are nights when other schedules interfere, but when the family eats together at home, their meal always concludes with prayer time.

Esther hosts Sabbath dinner for her family on Friday nights. As for me, I still say the prayer my mother recited with me at bedtime when I was little: "Angel of God, my guardian dear, to whom God's love commits me here; Ever this day, be at my side, to light, to guard, to rule and guide."

Each family is different. Think about a schedule that might work for you so you can pray aloud with your children at least once a week.

43. READ KID LIT

From time immemorial, people have learned life's lessons through stories. Many children's books convey spiritual messages in a way a child intuitively understands. Classics like *The Giving Tree*, *The Little Prince*, *The Velveteen Rabbit*, *A Wrinkle in Time*, or *The Chronicles of Narnia* all have a spiritual subtext. The velveteen rabbit's discovery that skin gets rubbed off in the process of becoming real is an allegorical reminder that nobody grows into full consciousness without some pain.

Read aloud to your children. And if you don't have kids, you might still read some of the great children's literature. The books are short, easy to digest, and you may be surprised at how deeply they touch your spirit. Be alert for the surprising message God may have for you within a simple children's story.

44. CREATE TRADITIONS

Many families gather at an advent wreath in December. My daughter's family does something more. They hold Tree Time in the darkened living room where only the Christmas tree lights glow. Sony has always liked to tell stories, and when her youngest son Danny was four, she spontaneously began a story about a country mouse who wanted to see Santa. As she spun out her story, Sony saw rapt expressions on both of her sons' faces. Even her husband was listening carefully. Just when the suspense was at its height, she paused and smiled. "To be continued tomorrow!" Sony continued her story night after next night until Christmas Eve. Her grand, satisfying finale brought "Ooohs" and "Ahhhhs" from her audience of three.

The following year, inspired by Danny's favorite stuffed animal, her story centered on Pete the Penguin. Though her boys are teenagers now, the family still gathers two or three times a week in December for Tree Time. Instead of a new story, Danny and Jake say, "Remember Mom's story about. . . . ?" And with smiles and laughter, they remind each other of earlier favorites.

There's nothing "overtly religious" about this tradition, but if the Great Commandment calls on us to love one another, what better way to express our love than by gathering regularly with family? What are the special traditions in your family? Make a small vow not to get so busy that you let them slide.

45. BE SILLY NOW AND THEN

My children's daddy had a great sense of humor and he never minded acting silly. On a road trip, he suddenly shouted, "Everyone who loves mommy raise your right ear!" In the swimming pool, he'd grab a kid and twirl around and around, churning up the water to play "Washing Machine." Out of his pocket, he'd pull a red clown's nose and start making faces. And our kids, along with their friends, loved it when he strummed his guitar and sang funny songs.

I still remember the day one little neighbor kid knocked at our front door to ask, "Can your daddy come out and play?" Not everyone is that sort of extrovert, but be careful not to become so rushed and harried that you forget the playful part of family life. Playing together can be as important as praying together. Observe yourself in the next few days. Are you finding a way to relax and be playful with your kids? Invite the Holy Spirit to help you lighten up.

46. LISTEN TO YOUR INNER WISDOM

Joan tells her fifth-grade students and her own children, "Your feelings have stories behind them, and if you get quiet and listen, you'll learn what they are." One day, her son David came home from school, upset because a friend had been mean to him. Marianne encouraged him to explore "the story" behind his anger. After a while, tears came, and David said, "I didn't think *friends* were supposed to do that." He had "listened" and discovered the *hurt* that lay behind his anger.

Psychologists have learned that anger is a secondary emotion that always covers up more primal feelings of hurt or fear. "God is as close to us as we risk being close to our real selves," Joan told me. "When children have the tools to experience the 'story' behind their negative feelings, they're able to process what's really going on and can usually release their feelings in a healthy way. I believe that helps them on their spiritual journey."

When negative emotions take hold of you, sit quietly and ask for God's grace to heed the story behind your feelings. Then let Jesus lead you to the place of understanding and release.

47. SIT WITH YOUR CHILD AT NIGHT

Not everyone has a small child, but if you do, spend a few minutes sitting in your child's darkened bedroom with your arms around your little sleepyhead. Your child will love it. Busy working moms are often so rushed as they move their children here or there that quiet touching time gets lost. As you hold your child, realize that you, too, are held by the loving God that Jesus described so familiarly as "Abba"—or "Papa." Place yourself in God's loving embrace.

PERSONAL BEHAVIOR

⏰ 48. BE ENTHUSIASTIC!

When I started looking for my first job, an advisor urged, "Be enthusiastic in whatever you do. Enthusiasm will take you further than any amount of experience." He was right. Think about the enthusiastic people you know. They can turn a boring drive into an adventure, extra work into opportunity, and strangers into friends.

"Years wrinkle the skin," wrote Samuel Ullman, "but to give up enthusiasm wrinkles the soul." Maybe that's because *enthusiasm* comes from the Greek and means "God within." One of the best ways to pray is simply to live enthusiastically. It will put a sparkle in your eyes, a lilt in your steps, and best of all, smooth the wrinkles from your soul.

⏰ 49. SPEAK TO THE STARS

When I worked at a greeting card company, I wrote this copy for the cover of a Christmas card:

*In the crisp, clear darkness of a December night
I look at the sky and ponder God . . .
Creator of an infinity of stars
Millions, billions . . . beyond any number I might count . . .
Is it not a miracle, indeed, that God
can look through the stars
. . . to me?*

I was 31 when I wrote those words, and at the time, I didn't believe any of them. Painful circumstances, especially the sudden, early death of my husband, had shattered my comfortable, taken-for-granted faith. I felt adrift in an existential universe that had no particular meaning. When I looked at the night sky, all I saw were flashes of light. I didn't see God and it sure didn't seem as if God saw me.

But years later, I realized that even though it *seemed* as if God had abandoned me, much of what sustained and strengthened me during that anguished period came through gifts of grace, sometimes accomplished in the actions of others.

Even if you're not quite sure you believe them, say aloud these words on a starry night: "Is it not a miracle indeed that God can look through the stars. . . . to me?" And consider that while God does look through the stars to see you, sometimes you must look past your own doubts to see God.

50. MEDITATE IN MOTION

Now and then, trade in your aerobics class or your TV-and-

Personal Behavior

treadmill for more solitary exercise. Walk. Run. Swim. Bicycle. Kayak. When I bicycle by myself, I pray with each turn of the wheels, as if they're prayer beads. On the shore of Lake Michigan, I spoke to a woman who had just pulled her yellow kayak onto the beach. Sitting low in the water as she paddles makes her feel connected with the universe, she said. She called the rhythm of her arms, as they lifted and dropped, her "paddle prayer."

51. Read a poem

Try it, even if you have never read poetry before. Read a poem you were required to read in English Lit class. It may speak to you in a startling new way, as T. S. Eliot did to me. Or sample a poet you are unfamiliar with. Many poems are prayers in disguise, as in these lines by Rumi:

> *Judge not the Lord by feeble sense,*
> *But trust him for his grace;*
> *Behind a frowning providence*
> *He hides a smiling face.*[5]

Memorize a line or two, and a poem will pray for you.

52. Drink and think

My friend Susan watched in terror as her husband reached down for a newspaper and suddenly clutched his chest. "If Medivac hadn't reached us so fast, Jack would be dead," Susan told me later. Her eyes widened as she remembered the close call. Then she murmured, "I nearly lost my husband before I realized what a fine husband I had."

As clearly as if she were standing beside me, I heard my grandmother's crumbly old-lady's voice: "You never miss the water until the well runs dry. Remember that, Barbara Helen." When I was ten, I thought she meant, "Drink more water." Now I know better. How many times have I splashed and gulped the cold, clear water of my life and failed to taste the gifts that were running unnoticed through my fingers? A friendship I took for granted . . . a spouse . . . the everyday joys that come in jelly jars and daisies.

Nutritionists recommend drinking six glasses of water a day. Today, every time you drink, think of a blessing you may have taken for granted.

53. PLAY!

Ever watched a six-year-old toss pebbles in a pond? She's not trying to accomplish anything. She's simply having fun throwing out her pebbles. When days are hectic and full, it's hard to let ourselves relax and let go. Even our exercise programs have goals attached: twenty minutes on the treadmill to burn 120 calories. Yet wise, old Solomon put it well: there is "a time to dance . . . a time to laugh" (Ecclesiastes 3:4). And I would add, a time to play.

Jesus (who was at a party when he performed his first miracle) said to his disciples, "Unless you change and become

PERSONAL BEHAVIOR

like children, you will never enter the kingdom of heaven" (Matthew 18:3). Watch a little child giggle and whirl in a delicious, delightful paroxysm of play. Give yourself permission, now and then, to follow suit. Just let go and have fun doing something that isn't hooked to a goal. Visit an art gallery. Lie on the beach and read a novel. Sit in the park and feed the ducks. Go dancing!

Grown-ups who retain a childlike delight in play seem to better weather life's storms. What better way to praise God than with some lighthearted play? Watch how it helps you sing a new song unto the Lord.

54. Write-a-check prayer

Margot tithes and says that any time she finds herself worried about money, she writes a check to someone less fortunate. Do it, says Margot, even though a frightened part of you says you can't afford to. As you write your check, admit, "I'm scared, God, because I don't know if I can pay all my bills, yet I know I have so much. I give thanks for my abundance." There is a spiritual cycle of giving and receiving, and when we practice living generously, our own needs somehow get met.

55. Be a conscious giver

Mrs. Astor—the Grand Dame of New York Society—was still, at ninety-six years old, personally supervising the dispersal of charitable funds through the John Jacob Astor Foundation. Yet she wasn't born to wealth. She grew up—as I did!—in a military family, and went through the pain of an early divorce, then the death of her much-loved second husband. All before she married into Astor wealth.

I don't have the Astor millions, but aren't all of us called to give generously of whatever we do have? For some, it might be money; for others, an intangible, like a smile or a talent for empathetic listening. Today, be a conscious re-gifter of the gifts God has lavished upon you. Watch for opportunities to give and you will find them in unexpected places.

56. CELEBRATE YOUR SKIN!

More and more, women and men are opting for cosmetic surgery, urged on by ads and reality TV shows. Botox® parties have replaced Tupperware® parties. One acquaintance of mine celebrated her fortieth birthday with a $10,000 facelift she charged to her credit card.

Yet at a recent gathering of women friends, I was struck by the beauty of four women who are fifty-five, sixty-two, sixty-five, and seventy-one, respectively. All carry in their faces some of the sweet furrows of age, yet I saw in Helen such grace and inner elegance; in Marian equanimity and the ability to roll with the punches; in Dottie a questioning mind and artistic eye; and in Leslie empathetic warmth and friendliness. Inner spirit transcends youthful skin. Today, do not waste one moment bemoaning the wrinkles around your eyes. Instead, acknowledge something about yourself that is beautiful. Name it aloud. Carry yourself joyfully, with warm

PERSONAL BEHAVIOR

appreciation for your natural God-given beauty. Make it your goal to simply look your best at whatever age you are.

⏰ 57. GIVE AWAY SOMETHING YOU VALUE

In the seventies, middle-class families believed "the good life" included a car, home ownership, a happy marriage, an interesting job, and the ability to send their kids to college; by the year 2000, according to a Roper poll, the good life required "a lot of money," a color TV, a second car, travel abroad, and a vacation home. Yet when someone comes into unexpected money—by winning a lottery, for instance—studies show that after a year, their "happiness" level returns to about the same place it was before the extra money.

Sometimes the more we receive, the greedier we become.

How many of your possessions do you really *need*? Which ones are you afraid to relinquish because someday you "might" need them? Give away something you value but no longer use, remembering this Scripture: "Do not store up for yourselves treasures on earth . . . but store up for yourselves treasures in heaven" (Matthew 6:19). How do you feel after giving it away? Lighter?

⏰ 58. TURN A SLOGAN INTO PRAYER

Remember the wonderful children's book *The Little Engine that Could*? "I think I can I think I can I think I can. . . ." What a tribute to the power of positive thinking! Still, sometimes relying on our own will just isn't enough. That's when you might borrow the advertising slogan discovered by Ed Hays, a gifted writer who has a knack for noticing the holy in unexpected places. On the side of a railroad car owned by the Atchison, Topeka, and Santa Fe Railroad, Hays saw these words: "**Santa Fe, All the Way.**" In Spanish, *santa fe* means "holy faith." So today, as you chug through your workday, instead of depending solely on yourself—"I think I can I think I can"—bring God along. When you encounter a really big hill or a very dark tunnel, pray: "Santa fe, all the way. Holy faith, all the way."

59. WATCH!
Ethical actions are what we do when no one else is looking.

Recently, I bumped a car's fender in a parking lot, and I wrestled with myself. Should I leave a note? It was such a small bump and *my* car wasn't scratched, though it looked as if the other car *might* be dented. But had I made it? Or was it already there? Finally, I realized that if I was serious about living a principled, God-centered life, I had to leave a note. Even if it pushed up my insurance rates.

It's easy to overlook small ethical lapses. Taking work supplies home to use. Keeping the extra twenty cents a clerk mistakenly hands you in change. Telling a "white lie" to save face. I've done all those things, but I watch myself more carefully now. Today, observe the actions you take (or are tempted to take), *especially* when no one else is looking.

PERSONAL BEHAVIOR

⏰ 60. MAKE A RED LIGHT CONTRITION

When you're in a real hurry, every light seems to turn red—have you noticed? Instead of giving in to impatience, use the moment to think about your day. Have you been rude, irritable, or in any other way not lived up to the best that is in you? Before you step on the gas again, say a prayerful, "I'm sorry."

⏰ 61. BE A NON-CONFORMIST

Corva doesn't just talk about peace. She marches against war. She organizes petitions. She writes her congressional representatives. She's an outspoken activist who lives her beliefs.

Fr. Richard Rohr, author, speaker, and founder of the Center for Action and Contemplation once said, "Saints often faced family and friends who told them to be satisfied with just being good, just obeying the Commandments, just going to church and leading a decent life. . . . Saints have to struggle with the temptation to conform to what is socially acceptable instead of reaching out for holiness."[6]

Corva would never call herself a saint, but Rohr might. Consider an action that pushes you beyond comfortable conformity. Publicly defend a deed that's unpopular but morally right. If no immediate situation calls for action, say this short prayer: "Give me courage to act when the need arises."

⏰ 62. ENVISION WATER DROPS

I was sitting on a California beach with my tow-headed grandsons, and as they splashed in the ocean shallows, I had a sudden insight. *I am part of a continuum. Others will come after me, as I have come after my forbears, and when I die, it will be as if the ocean has lost a single drop of water. The ocean itself goes on, just as the force of Life will go on through my grandsons and beyond.* And then it occurred to me: *Problems that loom so large in my life are merely light swells when viewed from the perspective of eternity. I'm a water drop, just a tiny part of the whole.*

The realization was a great ego-reducer. I felt profoundly humbled.

I thought I had discovered something new until I came across these words by poet Walt Whitman:

> *On the beach at night alone . . . as I watch the bright stars shining—I think a thought of the clef of the universes. . . .*
> *A vast similitude interlocks all,*
> *All spheres, grown, ungrown, small, large, suns, moons, planets, comets, asteroids,*
> *All the substances of the same, and all that is spiritual upon the same,*
> *All distances of place, however wide,*
> *All distances of time—all inanimate forms,*
> *All Souls—all living bodies, though they be ever so different . . .*
> *This vast similitude spans them, and always has spann'd, and shall forever span them, and compactly hold them, and enclose them.*[7]

Next time you turn on a faucet and watch the water drops spill out, practice a moment of oceanic consciousness. See yourself as a single drop in the larger ocean of God's creation.

63. Ignore "If only's"

I've listened to people chant their "If only's." "If only I had made another choice," they say, "my life would have gone in a different direction and I'd be happier today." Or "I'd have more money now." Or, "I'd be at a better place in my career." Well, maybe. But a different choice might also have put their feet on a path that included hardships and pain they have been spared.

Never waste time or energy on "If only's." Instead, as Ed Hays wrote, "[E]mbrace the reality of your life as the mysterious way God has chosen for you."[8]

Today, affirm: "I embrace my life as the mysterious way God has chosen for me. I embrace my choices as ultimately working for my good."

64. Look for bridges

During a weekend camping trip, I kept getting my feet wet as I crossed the small stream near our campsite. It wasn't until I had jumped across rocks several times that I noticed, downstream, a path and a bridge. Once I saw the path, I laughed out loud. "How did I miss it?" I wondered.

Isn't life like that? There in full view is some aspect of God acting in our lives, yet we don't see; we keep struggling, jumping over rocks, getting our feet wet, and ignoring the bridge.

Today, be open to the help that God puts before you. Look a little harder for bridges in your life.

65. Grow a square-foot garden

"It's called square-foot gardening," said my neighbor Steve, pointing with pride to the neat wooden boxes that made a brown and green mosaic in his backyard. A large traditional garden had seemed unwieldy and too big to handle; instead, Steve found he could grow all the vegetables he wanted by breaking his garden into neat square-foot boxes. I admired the way he'd turned a big task into something manageable.

Mother Teresa had a similar idea when she spoke of committing to Christian service. "I never think of crowds," she said. "I think only of one person." Some people do operate on a large stage (an inspiring example is Bono, lead singer of the rock group U2, who has used his celebrity on behalf of African debt relief). But for most of us, square-foot gardens are the way. Today, look for just one person—or one situation—that could benefit from a square foot of kindness.

66. Experience the COG in you

Kansas City minister Bill Hage once said that everyone is born with a God-shaped vacuum inside. Since Nature abhors a vacuum, we look for ways to fill it. Some people use money, expensive cars, big houses, powerful titles. Others cling to the wrong relationship, making someone else responsible for their happiness. But since the emptiness inside us is God-shaped, nothing but God can fill it.

For years, I tried filling my emptiness with "rights": associating with the *right* people, having the *right* possessions, pursuing the *right* career. I even called myself a DAR ("Doing All Right"). But it wasn't enough.

About ten years ago, I started meeting regularly with others who were "doing all right" financially but who were seeking something more. As we talked and prayed together, something shifted inside me.

I began to see myself less as a DAR and more as a COG—a Child of God. And like any good cog, I was just one part of a larger whole.

What are you throwing into your God-shaped hole? Is it your job title? Your investment portfolio? Alcohol? Your children's achievements? Instead of thinking that you're a DAR, be willing to see yourself as a COG.

67. BUY INTO THE KINGDOM

Next time you see one of these signs—"SALE! Buy one, Get one free"—let it remind you that God makes the same offer. It's right there in Scripture: "Seek first the kingdom of God and all else will be given to you." Ask yourself, "Am I ready to seek *first* the kingdom of God?" It's not cheap; Jesus called it the pearl of great price. Are you willing to get rid of all that you own—all the prideful "stuff" your ego carts around? Affirm, "Yes, Lord, I seek the kingdom." If the words stick in

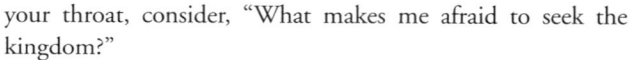

your throat, consider, "What makes me afraid to seek the kingdom?"

68. BLESS THE ANIMALS

In the wake of Hurricane Katrina, a group of sixteen animal lovers from my city drove to New Orleans in a large van filled with veterinary supplies. On their first trip, they rescued thirty dogs and sixteen cats that were abandoned in the city's flooding. I nearly wept when I read about their efforts.

Charles Philip Price, a minister, wrote this prayer:

*O God, you created all living things on the face of the
    earth and gave us dominion over them.
Grant that we may be faithful to this trust in the way we
    treat all animals, both wild and tame.
Grant that our use of them may be both merciful and wise.
So may we lend our voices to the praise of your goodness
    which endures forever.*

Ask God's blessing on all those who work with abandoned, hurt, and mistreated animals. And bless the animals, too.

69. LET HAPPINESS FIND YOU

When I taught freshman English at a state university, I asked my students to write a theme on one of their life's goals. It startled me how many wrote, "My goal is to be happy." Is it a function of youth to think you find happiness the way you find your car keys, simply by looking? Some of life's happiest

Personal Behavior

moments sidle in on cat's feet. They come quite unexpectedly.

I remember a moment while camping in the Sierras when I sprawled on my back, half-hidden in the grass of a high mountain meadow, my face raised to the sun, listening to my small children laugh as they fished with their father in a nearby stream. I felt so happy! Another moment occurred years later as I walked between my young adult sons. I looked up at one, and then the other—one 6'2" and the other 6 feet tall, both blonde and handsome, each taking long, confident strides—and my heart swelled with happiness. They'd made it! They were ready to face the world as adults and I rejoiced!

When we chase happiness directly, it often eludes us. We have to let happiness find us and then recognize it when it occurs. Think about some of your happiest moments. Were they big occasions or small? Expected or unexpected? Long-lasting or fleeting? What has made you happy this past week?

For all that has made you happy this past week, give thanks. You've been blessed.

70. Dance your prayer

Have you ever been home alone, put on a music CD, and then blissfully danced around your living room—bending, twirling, twisting, leaping—expressing yourself in way you never would if you thought someone was watching? I have.

"Dance increases the experience of the divine, and in many traditions, has been as much a part of religious expression as music," dancer Janet Weeks wrote in *Dance Magazine*.[9]

The Psalmist agrees: "Sing to the Lord a new song . . . praise his name with dancing, making melody to him with tambourine and lyre" (Psalms 149:1, 3).

I wish we danced more in church worship. Next time you're home alone, turn on some music, loosen your limbs, and let your feet, your arms, your whole body whirl in joyful praise to the Lord.

71. LOOK FOR GIFTS OF SERENDIPITY

Depak Chopra, the physician and best-selling author, tells a story about a car that picked him up for a ride to the airport. The car was bright yellow, an unusual color, so Dr. Chopra began looking for other glimpses of yellow, asking himself what yellow might mean in his life that day. The car drove past a bright yellow billboard advertising Celestial Seasonings tea. He took note, especially since this was a company Dr. Chopra wanted to contact about a project he had in mind. Later, on the plane, a man in a yellow jacket approached Chopra's row of seats and sat down beside him. Because he was alert to the color of yellow, Dr. Chopra spoke to the man. And he turned out to be an executive in the Celestial Seasonings Company, the very company Dr. Chopra wanted to contact.

If he hadn't been alert to the color yellow, would Dr. Chopra have spoken to his fellow passenger? Or, like so many of us when we fly, would he have hunkered down silently behind a paperback book and never glanced at his seat mate? Today, be alert to *serendipity*: life's small, unexpected gifts.

Personal Behavior

Sometimes we call them coincidences, but they're really not. When you have faith, you will find there is a reason for—and grace within—every single person who crosses our path.

Building Relationships

⏰ 72. Create a new image

Image advertising overwhelms us. Wear the right running shoes. Choose the right blue jeans. Drive the right car. The former chairman of office furniture company Herman Miller, Inc., Max Depress, said this about image: "I believe each of us is made in the image of God and comes into life with a tremendous diversity of gifts. Leaders build on what people are; [they don't try to] change them." What a wonderful idea: we are already cast in the right image, without enhancement of cashmere jackets or designer suits. Instead of labeling the people you meet, call all of them "God-holders." See the light of God shining through and notice how your new perception affects your behavior. Does it also affect another person's response to you?

⏰ 73. Learn to listen

Katie is a thirty-something attorney who works part-time

from home. Her schedule is very hectic. One day, when her five-year-old daughter ran in from outside, wanting her mom's attention, Katie started to say impatiently, "I don't have time!" Then she caught herself. "I took a deep, slow breath, and changed my tone of voice," Katie told me later. "I listened—really listened—to what my daughter said."

Most of us don't *really* listen. Usually, we're just waiting our turn to speak. (And maybe thinking, "Yeah, yeah, hurry up. I've got a better story to tell.") At least once today, practice "active" listening. Give your undivided attention to what another person is saying—not just in words but in body language, too. Revelation 2:11 says, "He who has an ear, let him hear what the Spirit says. . . ." Ask God to open your ears—and your heart—to really hear.

74. BE MORE ACCEPTING

Once, in the midst of a quarrel, my husband cried, "Why can't you accept me for who I am?" The anguish of that question immediately stopped me, for isn't that what all of us want? To be loved for who we are? But how can we accept another unless we first accept ourselves? For years, I held myself to an impossible standard of perfection, and if *I* had to be perfect, why, those I loved had to be, too. We can only love God and our neighbor to the extent that we love and accept ourselves.

Today, whenever you look in a mirror, make eye contact with yourself, and say aloud, "I love myself. Not as I will be. Not as I could be. But as *I am*." Did you believe the words you said aloud? If not, ask the Holy Spirit to aid you in greater self-acceptance. Then add these words: "I accept others as they are."

75. PICK A PRAYER PARTNER

Every week, Twila and her friend Helen meet for thirty minutes of prayer. After asking for God's grace in the words they speak to one another, they share how they have used spiritual principles in their lives over the past week. Then they discuss any problems that are bothering them. Lastly, they hold hands and take turns praying aloud, first for those on their prayer lists, and then for each other. "In the beginning, it seemed awkward to pray out loud with someone," admits Twila, "but now I'm convinced there's a reason why it says in the Gospels, 'Where two or more are gathered in my name there I am in the midst of them.' Praying together is very affirming. We rarely skip our prayer time together." Invite God into your midst. Say a prayer with a friend.

76. HOLD SOMEONE'S HAND

As soon as the gas station clerk said cheerfully, "Piece of cake, lady," I thought *Uh-oh*. That was what the last guy had said, five miles back. I'm one of those unfortunate souls who has *no* sense of direction. So I'm continually getting lost. I'm willing to ask for help, but alas, what I've learned is this: very few people give good directions. Usually they're so familiar with a route, and they forget a crucial detail.

Something similar seems to happen during a major life crisis. "Just move on," say well-meaning friends, but they often neglect to explain *how*. How do you move beyond the grief, anger, or sadness? Sometimes, it's best not to give directions, but simply to hold a friend's hand and say, "I know you feel lost. I'm here to listen."

God doesn't always give explicit directions, either. Here's where a friend who is willing to gently listen may act as God's instrument to help you discover for yourself God's subtle messages in your life.

77. BE NEIGHBORLY

My son's San Diego neighbors thoughtfully scheduled their tree-trimming on the day before he had his pool cleaned. That way, any excess mess flying into his pool would be cleaned up the very next day. That's the essence of neighborliness: noticing other people's needs and responding.

In my daughter's neighborhood, the Van Sickles go away for Thanksgiving, but their neighbors, the Halls, host a large family dinner at home. So the Van Sickles turn over the use of their kitchen, giving the Halls more space to cook the turkey and all the trimmings.

I loved what Kathy did for her nextdoor neighbor Kelly. When Kelly brought home her first baby, her husband was traveling a lot in his job, so Kathy, a mom several times over, wrote her phone number—"Big and bold!"—on a half dozen note cards and gave them to Kelly. "Stick these near every phone," she instructed, "so if you have an emergency or need information, I'll be easy to reach."

"Love thy neighbor" is at the core of our faith as Christians, but everyone is so busy today, neighborliness can fall to the bottom of our "To Do" list. One of my friends admitted, "I've haven't had time to even *meet* my neighbors." Think about something you might do this week to befriend one your neighbors. It could be as simple as tossing their newspaper from the end of their driveway up to their porch while you're taking a morning walk.

At the same time, keep in mind what Jesus replied when he was asked "Who is my neighbor?" He told the story of the good Samaritan. Stay alert today to ways in which you might broaden your definition of "neighbor."

78. CHANGE A HABIT

Let's admit it. All of us have certain habits that drive someone crazy. Sometimes it's something little, like dropping your towel on the bathroom floor, forgetting to return a borrowed tool, or leaving the cap off the toothpaste tube. Pick one habit that you know drives someone wild, and for the next three weeks, make a concerted effort to change. (Research has shown it takes about twenty-one days to change or adopt a habit.)

Now here's the real spiritual muscle-builder: if you do succeed in changing your bad habit, keep it between you and God. Don't go running to the other person to say, "Look! See what I did for you?" Your actions will speak for themselves.

⏰ 79. BOND WITH GENERATIONS

Clad in green scrubs and grinning from ear to ear, my son-in-law held out his swaddled newborn son. "Meet Jacob," he said. Gently I took my first-born grandchild into my arms. I looked from the baby to my daughter, still tired from giving birth. Surely it was only yesterday that I was giving birth to her. "You are the *child of my child*," I thought in wonder, caressing Jacob's tiny fingers. Abruptly I saw the connection, mother-to-child, mother-to-child, extending forward and back through endless generations, like a chain of exquisite prayer beads. Each of us, I realized, exists as a prayer to God, and by our very existence, we offer praise. Think about your own generational connections. Is there an older relative or a younger family member who would appreciate a phone call or a hug today?

⏰ 80. MAKE A THIRTY-SECOND CONNECTION

There is such a gift in simply being present with someone, even if the encounter lasts only thirty seconds. When I make eye contact with the supermarket clerk or the gas station attendant or the person I collide with as I rush into the elevator after lunch, my eyes say, "I see you. You are not a mere thing to me. You are not an appendage to the cash register. You are a person." It is false humility to assume we do not make a difference. Today, stay conscious of each interaction. Remind

Building Relationships

yourself that everyone you meet is a God-holder, and honor each person with eye contact and a smile. It doesn't matter if the person smiles back. You are offering a gift; not making a trade.

81. Practice a universal truth

If you think about it, there are only a handful of basic truths. They get repeated in slightly different ways, depending on the culture, the historical epoch, the religious doctrine, or the spiritual master. But the truths remain elemental and universal, and it is our life's work to discover and practice them. Here's my list:

- "Love God, not idols." (Not so easy in a society that worships money.)
- "Do no harm." (Avoid little murders of another's soul.)
- "Live truthfully." (Face life squarely without excuses or denial.)
- "Love your neighbor as yourself." (Stop being a perfectionist!)
- "Practice holy disengagement." (Stop trying to run your grown-up kids' lives. Give up designer-label clothing as a way to prove your worth.)
- "Surrender to God's will." (And to your bliss. Did you know they are one and the same?)
- "Wake up!" (Stop living on autopilot. Pay attention

to your life, moment by moment.)

Which of those truths is hardest for you to follow? See if you can practice it for one day. Notice when, where, and why it gives you the most trouble. Remember the old adage, "The truth shall set you free."

82. SCATTER FLOWERS

Thérèse of Lisieux did not live long (twenty-four years) or on a visible stage (she was a nun who died in 1897). But her autobiography, published after her death, made her known to the world, and she later was called "The Little Flower" because she believed love had to be proved in action, but not necessarily *big* action. She wrote, "That shall be my love, to scatter flowers—to miss no simple opportunity of making some small sacrifice, here by a smiling look, there by a kindly word, always doing the tiniest things right, and doing it for love."

Look for ways to scatter *your* flowers of love today, whether it's a smiling look or a kindly word.

83. HONOR YOUR CHOICES

I said good-bye to my mom, and hung up the phone, filled with guilty frustration. Once again we had disagreed about a decision I'd made regarding my teenage kids. *Why do I let her ring my chimes?* I wondered.

Jesus says, "You must leave your mother, your father, your sisters, your brothers, to follow me" (Matthew 19:29). That always seemed like a harsh admonition, but on this particular

Building Relationships

spring day, suddenly I got it. With my hand still on the phone, I said, "I am not my mother. I'm a different person altogether. I make different choices. And it's all right."

Today's experts use terms like "individuation" to mean we have to separate psychologically from our parents before we can live our own lives. With or without my mother's approval, I realized I was an adult and had to make choices that seemed right to me.

Two thousand years ago in Galilee, when Jesus said, "You must leave your mother and your father . . ." wasn't he giving the same message? Think about the relationship you have with your parents. Have you fully separated in order to become the unique person *you* are? Say a quick prayer to lovingly celebrate any differences you have. (And you might ask God's help in not letting your parents ring your chimes.)

WHEN TIMES ARE STRESSFUL

84. Walk in faith

One day, while feeling uncertain about a decision that would affect my long-term future, I wrote the following in my prayer journal:

*The path curves before me
hidden in parts,
So I do not see
Where it turns.
How easy to fear I will
Stumble or take a wrong turn.
Yet above the trees,
The sky is blue and sun-tipped,
And in the dazzling brightness
I step out in faith,
Knowing I will not stumble
For long;*

*Knowing that God is at my right hand
And at my left foot,
Above me as the dazzle
Below me as the humus.
And when I walk with God
I never walk alone.*

If you're wrestling with a tough decision, take a break and take a walk. Repeat to yourself as you walk: "God is at my right hand and at my left foot. And when I walk with God, I never walk alone."

85. Re-start your day

Have you ever had a day that starts wrong and goes downhill from there? You wake up late. Spill coffee on your suit. Run into a traffic jam that makes you miss a meeting with your boss. You feel stressed and irritable, ready to snap at everyone you meet.

Tom Jacobs, who leads yoga classes and prayer workshops, offers this bit of wisdom: "You can start your day over at any time." You do it in 3 easy steps.

1. *Stop.* Stop whatever you are doing, whether it's rustling through papers on your desk, scurrying down the hall, or picking up the phone. Just stop.
2. Take three slow, deep breaths, drawing in oxygen through your nostrils. Consciously fill your lungs as deeply as you

can. Slowly release your breath through your mouth. Notice how much more relaxed your body feels.
3. Say this prayer. "My day is starting *now*. From this moment on, I am living in the grace and love of God and his Son, Jesus Christ. Thank you, God."

86. BE OF GOOD CHEER

Opera star Beverly Sills achieved great fame, yet also dealt with private grief. Both of her children were born with disabilities. Sadly, her son, profoundly deaf, would never hear his mother's beautiful voice. Yet Beverly was so upbeat in manner that her nickname was "Bubbles." One day, an interviewer, referring to her nickname, asked, "How do you stay so happy?"

"Oh, I'm not always happy," she replied. "I am always cheerful. There's a difference."

Quite a difference. Happiness is a side effect. It happens to us. Something makes us happy. Cheerfulness is an *attitude*. It's something we can choose. It's not easy to put on a cheerful face in the wake of disappointment. But Scripture says, "A cheerful heart is a good medicine" (Proverbs 17:22). And it's true.

For the next twelve hours, no matter what the circumstances, prayerfully choose a cheerful manner, even if you have to "fake it 'til you make it." Notice how quickly your feelings catch up with your attitude.

87. Give up control

My youngest brother said to me jokingly, "Barb, you could retire from being our family's camp director." My quick response: "Rob, I'm the first-born. I was *raised* to be the family camp director." If you're an oldest daughter or son, you know exactly what I mean. We learned early to take charge and be responsible. We're uncomfortable when we're *not* in control and directing things.

But Anthony Bloom, a minister, put a different spin on the idea of control. He told an interviewer, "I never ask myself what the result of an action will be—that is God's concern. The only question I ask is, 'What should I do at this particular moment?'"

Today, stay alert to situations where you feel compelled to control the outcome. Ask the Holy Spirit to use you and to help you release your desire to control. Believe that if you act in the Spirit, the fruits of the Spirit will come. Maybe not exactly as you plan, but they will come.

88. Find the beginning

After my husband, John, died, I felt as profoundly shattered as my grandmother's vase, the one with the hairline cracks in it. It looked whole, yet one day, as I watched, it quietly broke apart into so many pieces. *That's just like me*, I thought, and felt a crushing sense of despair.

It's never easy to pick up the pieces after a profound loss, or the ending of one phase of your life. Yet sometimes it takes a shattering to humble us enough to let God's grace work in us, and we may only see God's grace in hindsight. In picking up the shattered pieces of my life after John's death, I found strength I didn't know I had. And I also discovered parts of me that I'd kept hidden—even from myself—because I hadn't needed them.

Think about an ending in your life. Can you see how it also marked a beginning? If you're going through an ending right now, can you trust that something new—and good—will come? If you can't, use these words from Scripture: "I believe; help my unbelief" (Mark 9:24).

89. LAUGH YOUR PRAYER

Did you know a hearty belly laugh sends the same amount of endorphins to your brain as ten minutes of aerobic exercise and can lower your risk of heart disease? Judy Goldblum-Carlton, a humor therapist at the University of Maryland Hospital says, "When you laugh heartily, every organ is being massaged including your heart, lungs and digestive system."[10]

During a sad time in my life, I decided it might help if I consciously cultivated my humorous side. Every morning, I prayerfully affirmed, "Oh Lord, today I am happy and cheerful. I have a *great* sense of humor." And I began looking for the funny side of life. I read the newspaper comics, something I hadn't done before. I started a "humor file" at work, and dropped into it cartoons and e-mailed humor that tickled me. (*The New Yorker* magazine is a font of great cartoons.) When a comedy played at a local movie theatre, I tried to go see it. We always laugh more when we're part of a group than when we're alone.

And I looked for humor in the ordinary. "Watching a crow walk is hysterical, and squirrels are natural comedians," observes Goldblum-Carlton. "There is so much funny stuff around you if you open your eyes."

Laughter is mentioned as far back as the book of Genesis, when Sarah says, following the late-life birth of her son Isaac, "God has brought me laughter, and everyone who hears will laugh with me."

Ask God to bring laughter into your day today. And if you can, share it with someone else.

90. YO-YO YOUR WORRY

It's not uncommon these days for mergers and downsizing to put jobs at risk. In Scripture, Jesus says repeatedly, "Be not afraid," but that's not always easy advice to follow. I went through a period of severe anxiety after twelve people were laid off at an ad agency where I worked. My friend Don, though he worked at a different agency, was in the same high-risk field. He gave me an unusual gift: a yo-yo. He said it was a replica of a yo-yo he owned. "Keep it in your desk and when you get scared, yo-yo your fear to God," he said. It was such a silly idea that I laughed, but after he left, I tried it. I coupled the action of the yo-yo with a heartfelt, "I send my fear to God."

When Times Are Stressful

At first, nothing happened, but gradually, as I continued to play—and pray—with my yo-yo, a sense of peace stole over me. When the anxiety returned a few hours later, I pulled out my yo-yo. For a few days, I must have yo-yo'd my fear to God at least twenty times a day, but gradually, it became enough simply to hold the yo-yo. I looked on it as a symbol reassuring me that, no matter what happened, God's loving strength would help me—and my family—get through it.

91. Look for signs of hope

My friend Howard teaches theater at a Midwest university, but he grew up in Australia " . . . where it's bleak and barren in the outback," he said. "There is poverty to the landscape. Yet in the midst of the bleakness, the most beautifully colored birds lift suddenly into the air, taking wing before you—as if God placed these richly plumaged birds as a sign of hope in the wilderness. We need to look for the winged colors of hope in our own personal deserts."

Yes, although sometimes, on days when I feel harried and strung out, it's hard to see the winged colors of hope. Or do they take flight so quickly that I fail to notice? Today, look for hope's bright plumage, even if your life has lately been a desert. Remember that we are most likely to see what we open up our minds to see.

92. Pick your halos carefully

Some people seem to lead such perfect lives. It's as if they're surrounded by an aura—a halo—that makes them "glitter when they walk." For me, one of those haloed souls was the executive vice president of the ad agency where I worked. Rob had the blonde good looks of a movie star; you just knew he'd never had a teenage pimple. He lived in a large home with a beautiful wife and three well-behaved children, and for years, whenever I hit a snag in my own life, I would say, with a touch of envy, "I'll bet Rob never has this kind of problem."

Then one weekend, Rob put a gun to his head and pulled the trigger.

In a hushed voice, the colleague who told me said, "It's like the poem, 'Richard Corey.'"

I recalled E. A. Robinson's poem from English Lit class, and realized that we never know what pain may hide behind the superficial façade of a person's life. Or, conversely, what joy a person might be experiencing who would seem to have little reason for joy.

Real halos come not from problem-free lives but from the grace with which we handle our problems. Have you haloed someone? Ask for the grace to be freed of envy, and invite God's blessing on the person.

93. Fix it or forget it

Over lunch, I was worrying aloud to my friend Barbara about a problem I faced. Like a dog worrying a bone, I couldn't let it alone. Finally, Barbara threw up her hands in exasperation. "Have you read your Bible lately? Over and over, Jesus tells his disciples, 'Have no fear.' Or, 'Do not borrow anxiety for tomorrow.'"

"Yes, *but*—"

"No *buts* about it. Look, I figure there are two times not to worry. Don't worry if the problem is one you can fix. Just go fix it. And don't worry if the problem is one you can't fix, because worrying won't change anything. That's when you hand it over to God."

Are you worrying about a problem? Which kind is it? One you can fix or one you hand over to God?

94. Fall gracefully

When my grandson Jake was learning to walk, I was fascinated by the process. He would pull himself up on the corner of a chair and stumble forward until—*plop!*—down he fell on his well-padded rear. Jake always looked surprised—"How did this happen?"—but he seldom cried. He just pulled himself up and tried again. After he fell three or four times, I chuckled, thinking to myself, "I wonder if Jake is saying in his little baby mind, 'Well, that proves it. *I'll* never walk'?"

Of course not. To Jake, falling was part of the learning curve.

God doesn't count the times we fall either. Say this prayer: "The next time I fall, O Lord, give me the grace to remember that it's just part of the learning curve."

You might also ponder: what have your falls taught you?

⏰ 95. Let go, let God

Lois was hospitalized with cancerous melanoma. She tried to pray, but her mind stayed trapped in the fearful words, "I don't want to die." Then a friend from church brought her a papier-maché clown attached to a parachute. "Here's your let-go-and-let-God clown," said Hank. Lois couldn't help it. She laughed, especially when Hank hung the clown on her I.V. pole, where she could watch him bounce up and down beneath his parachute. All through the next few hours, Lois looked at the clown with his silly smile and painted cheeks, and gradually peace replaced her fear. "I knew I wanted to live, and I hoped I would, but I let go of my need to control life's outcome."

Several years later, Lois is alive and well, the cancer in total remission. What if the outcome had been otherwise? "I had let go," Lois murmurs. Psalm 112 proclaims, "He will have no fear of bad news; his heart is steadfast, trusting in the Lord."

If you have lost your job or learned a scary diagnosis or heard your spouse say, "I want a divorce," it's pretty hard to feel confident and trusting. Don't even try to do it all at once, but do ask the Holy Spirit to help you let go of your fear. Release it for just one minute. Tomorrow, try to release it for two minutes. Continue extending the time in which you let go and let God.

When Times Are Stressful

⏰ 96. Release black squiggles and old dust

By accident, while looking through some family papers, I came across an angry letter my favorite cousin had sent me after a falling out we'd had. Although I had tried several times to patch up our differences, Dee refused to talk, so the issue was still unresolved. As I reread her letter, all kinds of sad, hurt, angry feelings surfaced. I was startled at their intensity. I loved my cousin and couldn't understand why she had never been willing to "kiss and make up." But after awhile, I thought: now isn't this silly? I'm allowing old black squiggles on a piece of paper to throw me into an emotional tailspin. It's not as if the letter writer is doing it because she doesn't even know I'm rereading the letter. I'm doing it to myself.

Then and there, I decided to stop. I crumpled the letter and threw it away so it wouldn't show up again, and quickly made a gratitude list of six blessings in my life *right now*. I prayerfully expressed sorrow to God for my part in creating the problem with my cousin. (Seldom is a broken relationship ever the fault of just one person. As Jesus pointed out, before looking for the splinter in another person's eye, examine the boulder in your own.) I asked God to bless my cousin and if possible, to give us both the necessary grace to restore our relationship. And finally, I remembered Jesus' advice to his disciples: "Shake off the dust from your feet" and move on (Matthew 10:14). Until another person is ready, that may be all you can do.

97. Look for the Fruit

For a long time, a Peanuts® comic strip hung behind my desk. In it, Lucy sits on a curb, looking woebegone, when Charlie Brown comes along. "Cheer up, Lucy, life has its ups and downs." Lucy jumps up and demands, "But *why*? Why can't life have ups—and upper ups?"

How I laughed when I saw that strip. "That's me," I thought. "Always looking for the Land of Upper-Ups where nothing bad or sad or scary happens." It's taken awhile to realize that life with only upper-ups would be as bland as a bowl of tasteless yogurt. The truth is, I've done some of my best growing during the down times. (Isn't that where we find the fruit in most yogurt? At the bottom?) And eventually, life curves up again. Next time you're feeling down, consider these lines from the Psalms: "Their hearts are steady, they will not be afraid. . . . Why are you cast down, O my soul, and why are you disquieted within me? Hope in God" (Psalms 112:8; 42:11).

98. Empathize!

We were doing knee bends in aerobics class when the cartilage tore loose in my knee. Whoeeee. *That's* when I discovered pain. Pain you can't ignore; pain so intense you will do anything to stop it. I've had two knee surgeries since, and rehab was tough. But it's made me more compassionate toward the pain of others.

When Times Are Stressful

When was the last time you experienced pain, either physical or emotional? What responses helped you tolerate it? Do you know someone who's hurting now? Examine your feelings. It's easy to dismiss another person's pain, or become impatient, even irritated; especially if the injury isn't visible, or if the pain occurs from a lifestyle choice. ("You have emphysema? Well, you were *warned* against smoking.")

Are you avoiding a person who is hurting? Are you uncomfortable because you don't know what to do? Don't be like Job's friends, who wound up accusing him: "Is not your wickedness great? There is no end to your iniquities" (Job 22:5–6). Pray for grace to be compassionate toward anyone who is hurting.

⏰ 99. Keep your center strong

Exercise is one of the best stress-relievers, and Pilates—named for the originator—has become very popular. The exercises, often done with the help of a large rubber ball, work on strengthening your core (diaphragm, pelvis, lower back, and buttocks). Joseph Pilates believed that if your center is weak, the rest of you weakens and becomes unstable until, eventually, you collapse in on yourself, causing problems to occur in your knees, hips, and lower back.

There's a perfect metaphor in one of the Gospels. Jesus describes two houses, one built on rock and the other on sand. When storm and wind arose, the house built on sand quickly collapsed. The house with a strong rock core weathered the storm.

Grace on the Go

People who want a strong physical core exercise regularly with their Pilates equipment. People who want a strong spiritual core need to pray regularly. Prayer doesn't always require formal words or a visit to church but it does require daily practice. It's why I'm writing this book.

The Reverend Martin Luther King and Mother Teresa, those two spiritual giants, both said that the busier they got, the more important it became to pray each day.

In the Evening

⏰ 100. Trade the 10 o'clock news for Vespers

Are you watching thirty minutes of violence—car crashes, murders, rapes, fires, all the stuff of evening news—and then going to bed? Researchers tell us that our subconscious may translate into turbulent dreams what we think about immediately before going to sleep. So trade in the news for Vespers: the Church's Evensong. Vespers is a thanksgiving prayer that looks back on the day just passed with all its redeeming graces—graces we've experienced while being on the go—and is fervently grateful. Initiate your vespers moment with quiet music, reading a few pages of a favorite spiritual book, or listening to a tape or CD by a spiritual speaker. A beautiful psalm to read at night is Psalm 103. It begins, "Bless the Lord, o my soul . . . " and concludes, "Praise the Lord all his works everywhere in his dominion." Now isn't that better than the violence of the news?

⏰ 101. Start a "Blessings!" Journal

Blessings happen every day if we open our eyes to see them. The first daffodil of spring. A rainbow after a storm. A friendly smile from someone you thought was mad at you. An unexpected check arriving just when you were worried about paying a bill. Writer Eric Hoffer said, "The hardest arithmetic to master is that which enables us to count our blessings"[11] and it's true. We're much more prone to add up our worries.

That's why it's so helpful to write down your blessings. Buy a notebook to keep on your bedside table. When you climb into bed at night, write down one blessing you experienced that day. Remember what St. Paul said? "I have learned to be content whatever my circumstances" (Phillipians 4:11). Reflecting Paul's sentiment, Rev. Norman Vincent Peale, in his life-changing book *The Power of Positive Thinking*, declared, "Happiness and effectiveness depend upon the kinds of thoughts we think."[12]

So start counting your blessings. On paper! Your inner and your outer world will change once you do.

*⏰ 102. Freshen your prayers

Repeating prayers we have always said can become so habitual that the words lose meaning. Now and then, write down a prayer you say frequently. Paraphrase it so you force your mind to look at it anew. For instance, one day as I prayed the Lord's Prayer, I was struck in a new way by the line, "Give us

In the Evening

this day our daily bread." I was used to thinking of bread as physical sustenance, something necessary for my body. But if we ask, doesn't God also give spiritual sustenance to strengthen us in times of adversity? "God give us each day our daily sustenance, physical *and* spiritual" was a new, deeper way to think about a familiar prayer. Once a week, say a prayer from another tradition. To find one, simply go to the Internet and Google the name of any religion plus the word *prayer*. Here is an example from Hasidic Judaism:

Wherever I go—only Thou!
Wherever I stand—only Thou!
Thou! Thou! Thou!
When things are good—Thou!
When things are bad—Thou!
Thou! Thou! Thou![13]

Another beautiful prayer is the one below, attributed to an anonymous Native American:

Let me walk in beauty
And make my eyes ever behold
The red and purple sunset.
Make my hands respect the things You have made,
And my ears sharp to hear Your voice.
Make me wise so that I may understand

The things You have taught my people.
Let me learn the lessons You have hidden
In every leaf and rock.
I seek strength,
Not to be greater than my brother,
But to fight my greatest enemy:
Myself.
Make me always ready to come to You
With clean hands and straight eyes.
So when life fades
As a fading sunset
My spirit may come to You without shame.[14]

*⏰ 103. Forgive All Adversaries

Never go to bed harboring bad feelings toward another. If it's someone in your household, go and say, "I love you." And maybe, "I'm sorry." If you're angry at someone who lives far away, read aloud the Twenty-third Psalm. As you read, substitute plural pronouns for singular and think about the one you'd like to forgive. We're so prone to look at someone we're at odds with as "other" or "enemy" (even if it's a domestic enemy). As you read this psalm, instead of saying, "He leads me beside still waters," say, "He leads us *both* beside still waters, He restoreth *both* our souls." You'll be surprised at the power of this reminder that all of us walk through shadowed valleys, and all of us are connected and loved by the Creator.

In the Evening

Add to it the Lord's Prayer, and really mean the words, "Forgive us our trespasses as we forgive others."

104. Practice nighttime TAPS

Relax into sleep with the TAPS prayers. Offer *thanksgiving* for the day's blessing. Show *adoration* for the Creator who has given us this incredibly rich universe. *Petition* for your needs and those of your loved ones. Express *sorrow* if you've hurt another in any way. Sleep well.

Part II:
If you Have a Couple More Minutes . . .

Time Out: A Couple of Extra Minutes with God

Sitting in silence with God is an old, old way to pray. "Be still before the Lord, and wait patiently for him," wrote the Psalmist (Psalms 37:7). As long as humans have sought God, they have prayed into silence, listening for the still, small voice of God. Jesus himself frequently went off to pray alone and quietly.

Unlike most of the ideas in the rest of this book, sitting in silence requires a certain amount of dedicated time. It's not easy to slow our minds and simply *be*. Our thoughts tumble about like a basket full of puppies clambering on top of one another.

But if you can sit in silence for at least ten minutes every day, the wriggling puppies in your mind *will* calm down, and gradually, a shift will take place within you. Nothing dramatic. You will simply find yourself more in tune with God.

This kind of prayer works best if you don't look at it as a goal to accomplish or a process meant to gratify you. Instead, see it as a gift of your *time* that you are giving to God. Don't hunger for results. Experience whatever comes.

If the soul keeps far away
from all discourse in words,
the spirit of God will come into her.[15]

As you learn to sit quietly for ten minutes, you'll find you are able to live more often in the present moment at other times. If praying in the silence is new for you, here is a simple ten-step process.

1. Sit on a chair, on your bed, or on the floor and keep your spine straight though not uncomfortably stiff.

2. Begin with a brief passage of inspirational reading. It helps get you "in the mood." Think about the words you just read. What do they say to you about your own life?

3. Close your eyes and begin taking long, slow breaths—what I call belly breaths—the kind that start in your abdomen and fill your lungs. Breathe in through your nostrils and release to the count of five through your slightly opened mouth. Breathe this way three times. You'll notice that your body has relaxed.

4. Breathe normally but notice your breath as it goes in and out. Our breath is such a physical way of *in-spiring* us, yet we take it for granted. Notice it now. In . . . out . . . in . . . out.

Time Out: A Couple of Extra Minutes with God

5. You may choose to mentally repeat a holy word or phrase as you breathe: *Jesus, Christ have mercy,* or *Praise God.* When your thoughts wander from your breath and your holy word (as they will), gently bring them back around. Don't judge yourself. Notice what happens in your mind the way you watch clouds drift across a summer sky. Notice . . . and let it go.

6. Observe the sensations in your body. Most of the time, we carry our bodies around like briefcases, hardly noticing them. Pay attention now. Do your shoulders ache? Is there tension in your belly or your upper back? Notice the actual sensations, not with a goal of changing them, simply to be aware.

7. If you hear sounds, listen to the sound vibrations: the soft thud of footsteps in the hall outside; the hum of air-conditioning; a dog's bark. Don't think about what they mean. Simply hear them.

8. Return your attention to your breath. In . . . out. Notice how your chest moves as you breathe. Have your thoughts wandered? It's okay. Gently bring attention back to your breath and your holy word.

9. As your ten minutes end, slowly open your eyes. Murmur this prayer: "Thank you, God."

10. Begin your daily tasks.

Notes

1. Richard J. Foster and James Bryan Smith, eds., *Devotional Classics* (San Francisco: HarperSanFrancisco, 1990), 231.

2. Jean Maalouf, *Praying with Mother Teresa* (Ljamsville, MD: Word Among Us Press, 2003).

3. Scott Peck, *Abounding Grace*, ed. Scott Peck (Kansas City, MO: Andrews & McMeel, 2000).

4. *Harvard Business Review* (September 2005). Emphasis mine.

5. William Cowper, "Light Shining Out of Darkness," original text by John Newton [and William Cowper], *Olney Hymns, in Three Books, 5th edition* (London: J. Buckland and J. Johnson, 1788), Book III, no. 15, 255; taken from Representative Poetry on Line, University of Toronto Press, 1994–2002, University of Toronto Libraries.

6. Fr. Richard Rohr, author, speaker, and founder of the Center for Action and Contemplation in Albuquerque, New Mexico.

7. Walt Whitman, *Leaves of Grass*, 150th Anniversary Edition (Oxford: Oxford University Press, USA, 2005), 207.

8. Edward M. Hays, *The Lenten Labyrinth: Daily Reflections for the Journey of Lent* (Leavenworth, KS: Forest of Peace Publishing, 1994), 97.

9. Quoted in Barbara Bartocci, *Meditation in Motion* (Notre Dame, IN: Sorin Books, 2004), 25.

10. Judy Goldblum-Carlton, quoted in Michelle Weinstein, "Laughter is the Best Medicine for Your Heart," University of Maryland Medical System website, www.umm.edu/features/laughter.htm, 2005.

11. Eric Hoffer, www.quotationspage.com/quote/9471.html.

12. Norman Vincent Peale, *Thought Conditioners* (Foundation for Christian, 1989).

13. Early Hasidic song, quoted in Frances Sheridan Goulart, *God Has No Religion: Blending Traditions for Prayer* (Notre Dame, IN: Sorin Books, 2005), 195.

14. Goulart, *God Has No Religion*, 102.

15. Abba Poeman, *Sayings of the Desert Fathers* in Barbara Bartocci, *Midlife Awakenings* (Notre Dame, IN: Ave Maria Press, 1998), 11.

Also available from Morehouse Publishing

Alive and Loose in the Ordinary

Stories of the Incarnation
By Martha Sterne

Through her gift of storytelling, Martha Sterne shows that the Incarnation is alive and loose everywhere you look, in the listening ears, kind voices, and loving hearts of people you bump into everywhere.

"The book teems with memories and quirks and acts of stunning generosity.... Her narrative is like that of Flannery O'Connor, only more daily and more accessible."

—Walter Brueggemann, Professor Emeritus,
Columbia Theological Seminary

"Martha Sterne beautifully helps us reckon with the surprising moments of incarnational grace that we would otherwise surely miss in everyday life."

—Peter Wallace, producer and host of "Day 1,"
and author of *Out of the Quiet*

Also available from Morehouse Publishing

Windows into the Soul

Art as Spiritual Expression
By Michael Sullivan

"God is the artist—the poet—of the world. Since we are made in the image of God the artist, each of us is an artist of sorts; each of us is a work of art! The disciplines of our art—silence, attention, compassion, fierce truth-telling and, love—help us celebrate the awesome joy and privilege of being human. This eye- and heart-opening book will help us be who we are called to be and will show us the way home."

—ALAN JONES, DEAN OF GRACE CATHEDRAL

"A new approach to prayer that guides us gently through our creativity to new insights and responses to traditional prayer themes."

—NANCY CHINN, ARTIST, AUTHOR OF *SPACES FOR SPIRIT: ADORNING THE CHURCH* AND *WISDOM SEARCHES*

"If you are willing to set out on a journey with an experienced and faithful guide, let this book become your companion. Michael Sullivan points the way with just the right mixture of insight, holiness, sensuality, and grace."

—THE RIGHT REVEREND J. NEIL ALEXANDER, BISHOP OF ATLANTA